I0901513

Slithering Snakes

TIGER Snakes

by Julie Murray

Dash! LEVELED READERS

1

Dash!
LEVELED READERS

Level 1 – Beginning
Short and simple sentences with familiar words or patterns for children who are beginning to understand how letters and sounds go together.

Level 2 – Emerging
Longer words and sentences with more complex language patterns for readers who are practicing common words and letter sounds.

Level 3 – Transitional
More developed language and vocabulary for readers who are becoming more independent.

abdopublishing.com

Published by Abdo Zoom, a division of ABDO, P.O. Box 398166, Minneapolis, Minnesota 55439.
Copyright © 2018 by Abdo Consulting Group, Inc. International copyrights reserved in all countries. No part of this book may be reproduced in any form without written permission from the publisher.

Printed in the United States of America, North Mankato, Minnesota.
092017
012018

Photo Credits: Alamy, Getty Images, iStock, Minden Pictures, Shutterstock
Production Contributors: Kenny Abdo, Jennie Forsberg, Grace Hansen, John Hansen
Design Contributors: Dorothy Toth, Neil Klinepier

Publisher's Cataloging in Publication Data
Names: Murray, Julie, author.
Title: Tiger Snakes / by Julie Murray.
Description: Minneapolis, Minnesota: Abdo Zoom, 2018. | Series: Slithering snakes | Includes online resource and index.
Identifiers: LCCN 2017939246 | ISBN 9781532120763 (lib.bdg.) | ISBN 9781532121883 (ebook) | ISBN 9781532122446 (Read-to-Me ebook)
Subjects: LCSH: Tiger Snakes--Juvenile literature. | Snakes--Juvenile literature. | Reptiles--Juvenile literature.
Classification: DDC 597.96--dc23
LC record available at https://lccn.loc.gov/2017939246

THIS BOOK CONTAINS RECYCLED MATERIALS

Table of Contents

Tiger Snakes

Tiger snakes live in Australia.

They are usually found near swamps and **creeks**.

Some tiger snakes are olive-green in color. Others are brown or black.

Their bellies are light yellow.

Many have stripes on their bodies that look like tiger stripes.

They grow to be about 5 feet (1.5m) long.

Tiger snakes have sharp **fangs**. They release deadly **venom**.

They eat birds and frogs. They also eat lizards.

Tiger snakes can live for 15 years.

More Facts

- Tiger snakes shed their skin a few times each year.

- They are good swimmers.

- If **threatened**, they will flatten their head and rise up.

Glossary

creek – a natural stream of water normally smaller than a river.

fang – a long, pointed tooth that is used to bite prey and inject venom.

threatened – feel unsafe or insecure.

venom – the poison that certain snakes produce.

Index

Online Resources

Booklinks
NONFICTION NETWORK
FREE! ONLINE NONFICTION RESOURCES

To learn more about tiger snakes, please visit **abdobooklinks.com**. These links are routinely monitored and updated to provide the most current information available.